BERNARD BAXTER

THIRTY POEMS

&

ONE OTHER

Note for Librarians: A cataloguing record for this book is available from Library and Archives Canada at www.collectionscanada.ca/amicus/index-e.html
ISBN 1-4120-9193-4

Printed in Victoria, BC, Canada. Printed on paper with minimum 30% recycled fibre. Trafford's print shop runs on "green energy" from solar, wind and other environmentally-friendly power sources.

TRAFFORD
PUBLISHING™
Offices in Canada, USA, Ireland and UK

Book sales for North America and international:
Trafford Publishing, 6E–2333 Government St.,
Victoria, BC V8T 4P4 CANADA
phone 250 383 6864 (toll-free 1 888 232 4444)
fax 250 383 6804; email to orders@trafford.com
Book sales in Europe:
Trafford Publishing (UK) Limited, 9 Park End Street, 2nd Floor
Oxford, UK OX1 1HH UNITED KINGDOM
phone 44 (0)1865 722 113 (local rate 0845 230 9601)
facsimile 44 (0)1865 722 868; info.uk@trafford.com
Order online at:
trafford.com/06-0947

10   9   8   7   6   5   4   3   2   1

Acknowledgments

Landscape photographs by Maureen
Campbell

Author photograph by Susan Bradley

Layout, page and cover design by
Tom Kristensen

PREFACE

These poems were written between 1982 and 2005. Some relate to places in County Durham and Hexhamshire, Northumberland where we have happily lived, and enjoyed the stimulus of talented friends; others recall people and events from the Cambridgeshire fenlands of my boyhood; others are contemplative: Denise, who is her own writer, contributes the final poem, which refers to a pivotal stage in our lives.

During the 1980's, we were both still heavily committed to our professional careers, and now regret how little time amidst other pressures we chose to set aside for writing (a solitary and introspective occupation that cannot be forced); subsequently "retired", we still wage ongoing warfare against an over-large, underdrained, excessively wind-blasted, moorland garden.

The poems are presented in more or less their order of writing. I don't expect ever to attempt a prose autobiography, because I should want to leave out more than I would care to put in – nonetheless, personal memories, observations, and philosophical reflections form the substantial basis of the poetry.

Other works include "John", the book for an opera, produced in Newcastle, "The Hexhamshire Mummers' Play" produced at the Dipton Mill Inn, and numerous articles, essays, play scripts, diversions and fantasies.

CONTENTS

Written in Holmside, Co. Durham, 1982 - 95

Written in Hexhamshire, 1995 - 2005

And One Other

Swallows Observed

When the swallows returned this year
we cut a hole in the garage door
for their access.

Previous years we used to count them in
before shutting up for the night,
confining them until a human daystart
hours later than their own.
One night by chance we shut the male out,
found him clinging
in early light
to the crack he could not enter,
agonised,
wings crucifixional.

Now they produce two broods each summer,
refurbishing first the nest above the door,
midseason shifting to the rear –
a change of fleas at least.

Our garage shields no cars –
is potting-shed, strung onions, garlic,
tools, hoarded wood,
rusty machines, pigwire,
general clutter –
in which we work, through which we stumble.

So these visitors devise ways
of coping with our unwanted,
must-be-tolerated presence.

Male swallow sways on tele-wires,
shooting out peals of data –
complex code
to appraise his mate within
of our varying degrees of threat;
choosing the moment,
she darts out
with his map of the battleground
in her head, at her wingtips.

And how they scream their young to utter
Silence!
when we enter ....

Both tease our cerberus,
longing to snap them out of the air
as they skim through her ears,
but the guardian leaps in vain.

Sometimes when both are feeding brood
in unremitting categoric mode,
their sentry system fails,
so that one exiting
squeaks in alarm
as we loom hugely in the doorway.
But a few ems of airway
suffice them for evasion:
at full dash swooping in
they skid to a halt
on a strip of air
retro-ing on hung wings, slide off,
circuit roofs, before ...

choosing the moment,
they hurl from sunlight
into dusky gloom, loop up,
lightly alight at their nest,
where a row of maws
like mini yellow bin-liners
awaits the thrusting feast.

Some dozens of days
these driven suppliers
cram and puff up their nestful:
then one morning the air is full of fliers
blundering a little
on experimental wings, short tails –
but speedily taking possession
of their birthright.
By day's end have skipped
from nestbound to skyfree,
anxious parenting shrugged off.

Now at night on garage beams
the family row blinks
when we turn lights on,
shuffles a little, secure above our reach.

Until parents' second nesting.

Then, although all meet at evening
upon communal wires in rows content,
parents and offspring ...
banned the young from garage comfort
once serious new brooding starts.

"Get out! Get out!" shrill the adults,
chasing first-family intruders
to excluded perches for the nights.

Second family repeats the cycle only faster,
seems to grow quicker,
is thrust into flight more tersely.
As August becomes September,
"Will they make it, these late-born,"
we wonder, "fledge, feather, mature
for that long journey?"

Finally, generations mingled,
dark backs, breasts lightly flushed with pink,
the great flock gathers on wires,
many from local nests we never saw.
Some days' soaring and lunging flight
about house and garden, nearby woods,
logging in memory where they will return.
One morning emptiness, the swallows have gone.

Without lodestone or radio beacon,
gifted beyond earthplodding man,
prompted by the rolling globe,
these gyronauts, instinctive voyagers,
flee our winter,
flit beyond the horizon of our imaginings:
will yet return pin-point
to their imprinted destinations.

Day Surgery

Arrive 8.30 at a temporary ward
in a temporary hut:
seven beds in a bulge
in a corridor.
Greeted by Sister, cheerful, bustling,
"That's your bed, undress, put on this gown,
it fastens up the back –
don't tell me
you can't reach the strings;
and here's your sexy knickers
which won't fit you
you're too big."

Wait.
Time unwinds, slow, slower.
On the far side of the bulge
two others in hushed voices
mutually agree they didn't sleep at all
last night for dread of today.
Cheerful chat seems indelicate.

Best entertainment is Sister
flipping through her papers
at her table, centre stage
in this theatre in the round.
She dominates with brisk
keep-them-chirpy chatter.
(By definition, day patients
have delta-double-minus brains,
and are three parts deaf).

"Don't ask me who's going when –
they've changed the list
three times today already;
the anaesthetist's phoned in sick,
they're trying to find the other –
and he had a heart attack
three months since.
Here's your consent forms –
sign them where it says "proceed"
or you'll get nowt done.

Oh, right, it seems you're first."

Climb on a trolley
(" don't think *we'd* lift you d'yer?"),
seem to float in a pre-med daze
along a mile of corridors –
F1 speed –
into a cramped anteroom –
gleaming white promises no nasty bugs –
where three/four masked nurses
rub cold hands, chatter
about last night's clubbing
and absence of desirable men.

One seizes my arm, palpates a vein,
"Nice fat one, this", inserts a line.
"Did you remember this morning,
to have nothing to eat?
Don't bother to answer that –
it's too late now anyway ...."

Conscious, I'm back on my bed,
emerging from a four-pints-of-beer haze,
pleasant.
In a bottle on the bedside table,
what looks like a small oyster,
hard, white and wrinkled.
Sister smiles: "They pumped that
outa ya knee fluid, good enit?
Take it home as a memento."

A trolley:
"No one here wants dinner, do they?"
"Yes, I do!"
"Well, you can then, but mind,
if you puke,
you clear it up, not me."

Time drifts ……. the crossword's done,
plot of the novel palls;
elderly folk on zimmer frames
creak past our beds
to a day-room with TV.

Sister's phone rings.
"Is who ready to go out?
Hang on I'll check. Not sure
which one's still bleeding.
Suzanne, is Mr. Baxter the bleeder?
No, sure? Right!

Your wife's rung to come for you.
Here's your list
of what you mustn't do,
and here's your exercises –
mind you must do them
three times a day, or else –
and here's your next appointment date.
Ta-ra then."

Answers on a Postcard Please

On the day that Auntie Con died,
the space probe COBE
reported back to its ingenious creators
that the known Universe did indeed
explode into being
fifteen billion light-years
down the wrack of Time.

To contemplate that annihilating paradox
is to ask the primal questions:
Why are we here? Where are we going?

What do we make of a single life extinguished
(gone, regretted, adrift in memory,
ever less visited)
in the context of the nightmare probability
of other intelligences
whom we shall never meet,
caught in the time-distance parallax
of retreating or cohering matter,
contact banning?

Do other sentient specks -
like us finitely fogged,
marooned in that thinly islanded ocean –
scan the tight lines
of their own constrained horizons ....
for what?

The sighting of some liberating sail
bearing that ancient First Sea Lord
who whistled up the primal
smashing and creating storm –
coming again at last to rescue
the broken fragments of his scattered fleet?

Note: COBE = *"Collector of Background Emissions", whose data reinforced the "big bang" theory of the creation of our local universe.*

The Magistrate's Tale

Sitting in Court one day
I hear a tale unfold:
he had been where he should not
she had cried rape, called the police.
Her current man at once sought out
and smashed him
who did not raise hands to ward off
accepting retribution was due.

Through his solicitor he asks for bail
admits deep shame for family betrayed
and lust – condoned by her –
but force it *was not*
was not.
At that he looks up briefly
otherwise slumped in misery

The Crown opposes, casting doubts.

The courtroom's full, but that is surely her
pale with lightish hair, her oval face intent.
A group of friends, her phalanx in support,
condemns in silence
silently urging the Court commit.
And there his wife
face grained with the agony of this
grips hard a plastic shopping bag.

Beyond these neatly packaged facts
lies what fleshed truth?

.... She lives in a terrace sloping to the Tyne
where each house looks over other's shoulder
leaning on down
so you'd think the lowermost
would never hold the others up:
six parallel straight streets
corporately named
left bare in a bulldozed landscape.

Her partner on late shift
wakes midday
resentful of his pounding head
goes off in surly silence.
She smokes, chats with a drop-in friend,
feeds baby, yawns the evening through,
goes up to bed at ten,

as another man turns down her street –
dim-lit, rain brightening the cobbles
(should be backing music here
to pluck expectation) –
he stops by her door,
taps without answer,
thinks to test the latch,
finds it open, enters
- at his peril, he *must* know it -
not drunk but enough to blur
the edge of reason.

They've known each other since school,
flirted, danced together, drawn away.
Alerted by sounds

in dressing-gown and mules
she comes downstairs
is only part surprised.

The time is apt .....

Her man returns
tired from shift –
a shadow slipping out
and other signs –
he throws the hooking question
with the blow.
Terrified,
violation is her cry .....
in truth or mere defence?
Herself wronged
or need to convince?

Only she knows
perhaps not even she is sure:
reluctance? something misconstrued?

....The Court decides,
bail is refused, he's led away
not looking up, her guardian group
gather to leave, relieved.

Into which pause –
low enough but all can hear –
bitter quiet his wife to her
"Got everything you wanted then?"

Inner Window

When the graphs, X-rays, reports
left no doubt about the condition ....

"I feel so sorry for myself," she said –

a strange and poignant thought,
as though an entity may split
into two parts,
one observing the other with compassion
itself untouched by the malaise
that prompts the pity .

As in Maupassant's story
the fisherman sadly
follows the tiny coffin
containing his own severed arm
his brother could have saved.

Physical messages of pain transmit
to the same mind that registers
psychological outrage
for the damage done, pities
its other self for the trauma,
valuing its own existence.

Sadness for others' pain is a kindness,
but this secret encouragement
of ourselves
gives dignity and solace
to our only, lonely journey.

Teaching Practice

I observe …the student of course, but -
though long-unwashed windows -
spiked urban playground fences
beyond which, a flat dash away,
are rows of identical
houses, each with its tele dish;
mainroad hoardings
tall chimneys
flat-roofed jerry factories,
pylons behind under
a circumscribed city sky.

A hundred seagulls hunt
on landlubber legs
over rough grass.

In 3C's classroom sit or roam
a score of young teens
who, on the whole
while not feeling strongly about it,
don't really want to be here,
wish rather they were seagulling
round familiar streets
testing the boundaries
of their more vital lives –
but consent reluctantly to do
more or less
what the trainee teacher requires.
A compromise really.
They do just enough

to satisfy the cursory sweep
of his general gaze –
he hasn't yet acquired
the master's eye –
leaving plenty of space
for neighbourly chatter.

I sit at the back with my notepad.
Jo-Ann, tall with a single plait
rings on eight fingers
asks me what colour her eyes are –
she has to write this poem
describing herself:
not practising flirtation yet,
just restless, cannot bear
the isolation of quiet contemplation,
has a need to talk.

The trainee teacher, dark-haired, brisk
keen to do well
roves the classroom
uneasily aware of the difference
between his vision of pupil creativity
and the banal reality he's pulling in,
pauses with individuals, commends, suggests,
can't quite pinpoint
the spurring advice he should give;
while 3C ripple and chatter around him.

Like a becalmed helmsman
he knows his wished landfall,
can't catch the breeze to reach it.

Outside the windows,
a hundred seagulls
for no palpable reason
launch screaming into the sky
fly a half circle, subside
to their never-ending foraging.

Actually no freer
than the classbound children.

Both subject to instinctive responses,
conforming group behaviour of their kind.

Requiescat

"A sad life," some said
when Malcolm died at 53
drowned in alcohol and despair.

Not easy to be gay and partnerless
to have suffered cancer
dreading its return;
few close family, these dying early;
too gentle for career success;
deserted at the last
by the man he most looked to.

Possessed of unassuming talent:
to conjure illusion in a stage-set;
find beauty in flowers,
buildings, books.
Thoughtful, ruminative, kind.

Many mourned who valued him.
Many who mourned
valued him too late.
He had too much of loneliness.

What Was and Is

At Colmar in the musee Unterlinden
wondrous altar panels beam out
their images as bright as ever they did
in the dark ages of faith.

Wander through rooms
that lead to Issenheim,
see medieval faces
imposed upon familiar stories.

Christ prays in the Garden
his exhausted disciples asleep
while a coarse-faced posse
creeps up under cover of rocks
to make the arrest;
hook-nosed Judas leading
motions them to advance.

A crowd of the crude and cruel
bite their thumbs shouting derision
at Christ standing quietly under charge
of a confident self-contained officer
sharp in a green coat with gold facings.

At a crucifixion everybody's aunt
smart in a black coat fringed in orange
her hair well-ordered
beneath a sequined hat
looks on impassively.

St. Catherine awaits her martyrdom kneeling,
as a silver-coated executioner
with a large codpiece
swings his sword full-circle
at her slim neck,
above is a burning wheel
edged with knives,
beyond two red angels
carry off a virtuous soul to its reward
in a kind of hammock.

Before a cavernous lair
piled with human skulls
St. George well-armoured, calmly professional
sights down the length of his lance
thrusting into the dragon's maw;
his horse looks stern
stamping around the monster;
the dragon bloated and scaly
no match for the technology
brought against it, submits.
The sacrificial lady
sits prettily apart
hands neatly folded in her lap
detached apparently unmoved.
From the battlements of a toy castle
confounding perspective
enlarged king and queen,
her parents, view the event –
mother points to the drama,
father seems rather pained.

But Christ crucified
centrepiece of the Issenheim retable
moves the mind to wonder and despair.

He was familiar with death
this medieval master:
Christ is utterly, pitiably dead,
exhausted, defeated,
body dragging down
on stretched and tortured arms,
head sagging below the shoulders,
tongue protruding between bared teeth
greying lips drawn back,
the flesh so savagely torn
thorns hooked into the head
skin broken suppurating.

No doubt, no room for error:
Grunewald in passionate creation
knew that his Saviour died
understood the hideous process
every effect on nerve and sinew.
Knew with absolute certainty
this flesh could never
rise up in life again.

Yet knowing this
he then portrayed the risen Christ
floating free of the encumbering earth
renewed perfected upward borne
in a golden circle of light
mystical promise of re-creation.

Not for Grunewald the stylised figures
conventional statements
of some anodine faith.
From pain and elation
fear and hope observed
in the faces and fashions of his time
the paradox is posed:
Godhead and corpse,
prophet destroyed and eternal Lord.

Painting in faith
he left the centuries to choose.

High Points in France

Auvergne

Among the dead volcanoes
pragmatic roads hairpin and elbow
around, up; unedged tarmac
suffices two cars to pass,
but a metre outwards drops unguarded
dizzying downwards
to diminutive fields, hedgerows
on the valley floor.
No problem, local drivers
throw their one thousand cc cars
at bends in uphill slalom
until they reach the col
where four valleys fall away
through tree-clothed distance;
where a café sells
- as well as a menu at F80 -
whole cowhides,
great knuckles of smoked pork,
everything a tourist needs.
By Puy Mary, an eagle
chestnut-backed, black-winged
against deep-blue sky,
rides the thermals, shifting course
accurate as a spacecraft flipping
with precise tail angles.

On the tops
vibrato grasshoppers scrape tunes –

little green ones with brown rears,
larger maculate tawnies –
power their passionate paths,
jump-flying among low wiry growth –
an infinite string-section
serenading vast warm slopes.

Housewife with tined scoop
thrusts among straggling bushes
collecting blueberries.
Low dianthus, thyme, viola,
blue scabious brighten the grass-thatch.
While indefatigable moles
even here on the roof of France
throw up fresh hillocks as we tread.

Clinging halfway down
in a hamlet of a dozen elderly houses,
throwing dusty, long cool shadows,
is a plain, rubble-stone church.
Almost tread upon
a silent lady at prayer,
unmoving as the statues round the walls,
painted in the pastel blues and reds
of local piety.

The valley bottom is cow country
landscape rubbed and grazed
by man and cows
for cows and man
in eccentric fields
defined by rocky levees

and long farming practice;
electric wires snarl off
few cows in a patch of grass,
shifting grazing constantly managed.

Call to buy milk
at the tail end of a byre
in a pungent farmyard, where a small boy
pees among the cowpats
by buildings unchanged in decades,
but now pulsing to the teat-clusters
glass jars steel vats
of a tubercular–conscious age.

Jura

On French motorways 300km
absorb merely two hours of life –
speed-limit as fast as you can
or choose to go
without a trawling, predatory
cop in sight – swooped past
by black flocks of bikers –
through countryside anonymous
not France just anywhere,
until a last *peage* releases us
into the high Jura, where .....

on a rolling plateau, forested,
pre-Alpine villages promising
winter snow sports, but
broad meadow views now, still

on gentle sun-faced slopes.
Dwellings not crimped together
in conformist blocks
(see Anglo-Saxon LA rules)
but pleasingly set down randomly
where people wanted them to be.
Frontier country, this,
preparing in September for a long winter,
hot, clear-skied now in dying summer.
At every house are building
foursquare blocks of winter logs.
This weekend, a wedding celebration
takes up two full days:
behind an outdoor table
built for a hundred to sit at,
huge joints at 8 am are gently roasting
on long spits.

Through working forest roads
where huge blocks of trees
are colour-coded for the chainsaw,
great stacked trunks await vast *camions:*
sawdust, crushed bark, sharp resin smells.

Cevennes

Cool mornings, fierce midday sun –
not even the vine rustles
over our cold *apres midi* beers;
nothing stirs but lizards
darting with flicking tongues up cracks
to lie out immobile on baked surfaces.

Old ladies softly shuffle
from family farmhouse lunch,
salute us kindly,
creep through wallish gaps
up rough steps by dusty paths
to their narrow shuttered quarters
to siesta under a huddle of shingled roofs.

Heat presses down heavy as gravity

till dusk softens the sharp edges
of fragrant sweet-chestnut trees
on steep valley sides, goat-milking time,
when the old ladies are drawn back
by lure of the evening meal,
carrying posies culled
from tiny gardens clawed out of rock,
bright with tomatoes, and,
stretched out on rocky ledges,
pumpkins bronzing into ripeness.

Epergne

Cheerful auberge in small country town
at grape-harvest time
with a disused mill and houses
built to the very river edge:
families relax noisily
over long evening meal,
week's work over.
At the best table an older couple entertain

their large family and friends:
chief man barrel-bellied, huge-muscled –
short-sleeved shirt and straining belt:
no doubt a power at work,
but quiet under his wife's eye
who dominates talk,
keeps it up all night.
Their adult daughters –
can't miss the resemblance –
sharp-faced, quick to laugh,
flanked by husbands who say little,
but address themselves earnestly
to food and the rose wine,
reordered and replaced again
till the pink flushes all their faces,
reddens father's neck.

At mother's shoulder, solicitous,
perches Madame of the auberge
like a crow on a branch,
unmoving, quick-eyed, uttering
an occasional caw.

Withdrawn at an alcove table,
two stout English ladies,
one with brown hair sheared like a helmet
the other greyer, softer;
both wearing sweaters,
full skirts, sensible sandals –
respectable, confident
in their small but accommodating French.
Travel books, guides,

lie among the dishes
and a careful half-bottle of white wine –
"Histoire des Fenetres Roses,
Cathedrals de la France,
Environs de Paris", Guides Verts
and a scatter of maps.
Both make lengthy diary entries
as they eat, refer to sources,
record an enquiring day.
They pay *l'addition* in cash,
sharing the change
after serious consultation,
enter amounts in pocket books,
leave smiling.

What did you do in the War, Dad?

I joined the Wavy Navy
in nineteen-forty-one,
went to sea in a crab-pot
christened LCT 581,

a shallow-draught box
with a big bow-door
to drop on a beach
and send tanks ashore.

On the night before departure
the Liberty Boat was full –
men getting rid of surplus beer
in the two ways possible.

Sailing out of Portsmouth
on a grim and steely day
I was bitter sick for days on end
as we lurched across Biscay.

Halfway over the engines crashed
in a stink of burning oil:
we wallowed in an empty sea
two days of cursing toil

to find and build replacements
strip out and clean all down
in ways not found in the manuals
on the fitters' course at Troon.

Rejoined our slow flotilla
steaming in line ahead,
when the ship in front blew up (a mine?)
we took its place instead:

which made the SO's signal
bright as the fogbound day –
"Enemy subs on the surface
shall be rammed without delay."

From Gib. along North Africa,
Algiers, Sousse and on
past unfamiliar places
where the Desert War'd been won,

on to our embarkation point
place of sewage, stink and flies;
and there our massed armada
took on men, machines, supplies.

Bore them to enemy shorelines,
put down on Sicily;
we anchored off cleared landings,
swam in pellucid seas.

Followed two months' constant steaming
ploughing the wine-dark seas,
shifting equipment mountains
like labouring Hercules.

Malta – Sicily – Malta run
endless pall of diesel burn
heat and flies and engine din
as we go as we return.

Sometimes to cafes, trams and mosques
on the coast of Africa.
There naphtha flares heat pungent food
in back-lane souks near where

in wealthy streets poor urchins,
black eyes and woolly heads,
clamour all day for backsheesh
rags for their pavement beds,

grab at our passing trousers
spit on our boots and say,
"shoeshine look sah, jock jack,
shoeshine bugger must be."

My old tub leaves for Italy
on the next invasion shift:
I report to sick-bay
at the very hour they left.

Three months in Army hospitals,
a real nap hand I'd caught:
dysentery, boils, malaria.
sick paws, rashes of very sort.

Came home a commissioned officer,
resumed family life and pride
My health completely undermined
aged forty-six I died.

*Note: this ballad, based on my father's letters
home from his part in the Sicily campaign WW2 –
he was Motor Mechanic (known in the Navy as
"MM" = Mickey Mouse) in charge of the engine
room in an LCT ("Landing Craft - Tanks") – was
set to guitar music, recorded and sung by Jim
Gibson of Peartree, Co. Durham.*

January in the Shire

Wind builds snowdrifts
carving sharp creases
lines of beauty
quiffs and sideburns,
fragile to plunging invasion
by our leaping, floundering dog
nosing cock pheasants
with indignant squawk
from unlikely concealments,
while we lurch through
covered heather, roots,
beneath conifers whose loaded branches
drag down over Devil's Water
rolling glaucous and dark
between white-encrusted boulders.

In bleak light, rabbits
bask and lightly leap
on gleaming banks under hedges,
careless brown targets.

A bright bird marches
with deliberate strut
across yesterday's field.

Behind the house
thrushes and blackbirds
puff and bulk their feathers,
competing with chaffinches
in pursuit of scattered crumbs.

Grains of snow drive under eaves
into lofts, melt through ceilings;
blown snow fills tracks
levels hedge-tops.

Confined within this isolated house,
primitive nightmare grins
through windows at
our cocooned
comfortably serviced existence.

February

Frost tightens earth, crisps water,
slows green growth –
never entirely halts it
even in hardest winters.

Already paired robins, blackbirds
are flitting under shrubbage,
intent; careless even
of our black Lab's hunting,
thrusting his front-row shoulders,
looking to grab;

on his customary lope,
in unfettered, investigative mode,
checks the carnage
of car-battered corpses
down our fur-lined roads.

Life rhythms slow
in these between-perhaps times:
lambing approaching,
grass unmowable, soil unworkable.

Yet, sweetest of frosted veg,
parsnips and sprouts,
artichokes, cabbages
promise next season's plenty.
New garlic and rhubarb
probe upwards.

44

March

Only ribbons of snow remain,
few ragged heaps of waning drifts;
ditchwater races downhill,
spilling across roads:
dog joyously swimming, ducking,
vaulting out, shaking
and plunging again;
from his fifteen-inch eye-level
walls, fences,
crackling stems of last summer's
willow-herb, define and confine
his hunting space.
So field gates are his five-barred
windows on the larger world,
through which, lasciviously,
he eyes up sheep,
assesses the menace of a tup advancing,
froths with excitement at
collie-bearing quad-bikes,
from which wise bitches
snarl and snap dismissal
of his hopeful "surely me?" advances.
Usually, a brace of raucously
indignant grouse skim off a few yards,
reluctant pheasant is nosed
from its ground- hugging hide,
rabbit or hare slip silently
through well-known gaps in walls.
Great hunter is every trip hopeful.

Cold Spell into May

Low clouds, brown ragged skirts,
lie on the fells like smoke,
air dampens face, drops
penetrate cuffs and neck.
Grass I toiled to mow
has leapt up behind me,
flowers that yesterday glowed
in perfumed sunlight
now shrug down into cover.
Frost is forecast, so tonight
I must pull earth over
dark, flat potato leaves.

Late November

Sun glows muted red
declining into the hilltops
as our new black dog
charges through wiry heather
towards calling grouse
incautiously skylined.

My doppelganger shadow
strides beside me, reflected
along drystone walls;
almost-ever-here
hammering wind
is down, rare silence holds all calm.
Valley nods under blue sky –
only slowly change
drifting cloud pictures:
shoobunkin flowing tail, bull head,
Gulliver's flying island,
protean monsters,
sea spume, ragged foam.
Dog joyously greets,
licks muzzles of,
rescued Exmoor ponies
grazing a weedy swamp
heads curious over field gate.
Familiar farms tuck
tight under hillsides,
white blobs are dotted sheep.

Chapel cars and Sunday silence.

Foot and Mouth, 2001

Silent, unprefaced
crept in the plague,
infecting sheep and beasts.

Riding the breeze,
bird or badger borne,
nestling in nostrils,
on feet, in faeces,
contiguous contact?

How came the plague
does anyone know
is anyone telling?

Shrouded in white
grim phantoms appeared:
in bloody reality
emptied the meadows,
took away pride,
negated purpose,
destroyed creation -why?

Ask of God His
inscrutable purpose.

On Reading Japanese Short Stories of the
Nineteenth and Twentieth Centuries

Sadly depressing that
even our best fictional creators
produce such unfulfilling images
of alternative lifeforms, given
the unrestricted time, distance,
conformations they have
to work with, within or without.

Early in human social myth,
"anon" postulated God
creating woman out of
Adam's rib –
amazing early cloning forecast
that – so why have our
most ingenious inventors since
proposed no wonders
more exciting than dubious insect-headed,
oddly-bumped, alien scarecrows
from their impoverished imaginings?

Look no further than
diversity on Earth.

Our languages alone
are a shaken cup of wonders:
classic orders, scattered phonemes,
alphabet pictures,
light sounds, gutturals,
accents, dialects –

all fluxing, moving, living,
instinctive, easily accessed
locally by familial or foe?
(but distance their cliffs,
their faces become difficult to scale).

So.
Kojima Nobuo, Endo Shusaka,
and your teeming other minds,
consummate writing dynasties,
linking intelligences with
who can number how many
tribally diverse creators -
given that, in fractured tele-paths,
they must lose so much
subtlety of phrase, innuendo,
mistily transferrable perception?

Even so.
These Japanese mores
shock, challenge our received concepts:
of suicide as an expected,
inevitable, unavoided,
even welcomed payment for
deliberate or rash misdoings,
embraced by villains,
heroes, ordinary citizens,
the *amende honourable*,
necessary cleansing, personal forgiveness –
even with its formal, grisly,
traditional methodology;
of the socially enfranchised

life of brothel girls,
weighing up offers of marriage
as a stock-in-trade,
sometimes happy, often sick,
and never an indelicate reference
to the unsubtle practices of their trade;
of the stoic, physical endurance –
on the run, fright induced -
of forced guilty journeys
over mountainous terrains
with no chance of a fortunate outcome,
carrying if they must
their afflicted on their backs;
of the barber
famed for his skill
in never razor-nicking
the most delicate
or pustulated facial skin, who
suddenly afflicted wth a fever
and a coarse, complaining customer
... simply cut the fellow's throat.

What we strangely call "our Universe" –
though it's palpably no more
than a limited perception
of an infiniteness
we are not gifted to comprehend –
may, in its ending, expand
beyond rational connection,
or implode
in heavy gravitational demise,
or implode then bounce back

to an unquizzable renewal.
Such are some guesspels peddled
by smart astrothinkers:
but what galactic honest bookie
would bother to chalk up the odds?

Our cobweb of words –
treacherous and sticky
with its invaluable
lurking and murderous spider
drawn from all continents
and islands of this limited Earth -
this I'll bet on, favourite
to formulate best truth
for the outcome of our race.

Be Brave my Lonely

There is no knot
that cannot be untwined.
How long shall love endure?
When nature first bewrays us
and logic loses hold,
affection binds, oneness declines:
so it appears that two-in-one
the trinity reflects, and justifies
the ways of man to god.
But twining tests the structure:
it binds but pulls apart –
in crisis it's the integer
that stands, must stand, alone.

Absolve

The chances that offer
the choices that drive,
the wishes that beckon
those hopes that survive

both help in forgetting
suppress fear of forfeit
give power over weakness
the strength to survive.

Timor Mortis

Creation is storm-burst
though cradled in tender wrack,
torn, pierced, released
in surge of ecstatic pain:
new life is, despite coding,
snatched out of accident.

Strengthen then your heart.

Consulted? No. Existing, why?
I did not ask for birth.
Alive, my senses all conspire –
endure for ever's their desire,
the driving drive to live -
and grieve the certainty of death,
such waste of wisdom harvested,
but know because I am, then was,
I shall be senseless in eternity.

Meantime, strengthen my heart.

Quite futile to complain against
the great Cartographer,
when on his everlasting map
in his Recorder's clearest script
we're mimeographed and docketed.
We can appeal no higher court.

So strengthen all our hearts.

Words

8 am Prayer Book service,
sparsely congregated church,
runic words
drop into contemplative quietness;

so rubbed and rounded
by repetitive chorus –
like rough stones
rumbled in a jar
to make bright necklaces –
these ancient repetitions
have become
benevolent familiar echoes.

No matter they
formulate laws from a
social order before we fatally
ate fruit from the tree
of scientific infallibility
and learnt there is no truth
beyond provisional data –
they are old friends still;

words

usually are debased, abused,
commonest whores on the block,
trivialised below
brute communication
but for me,

words are the looking-glass,
the magic wardrobe,
the only key completely able
to unlock feeling, perception

words
sinuous elegant diverse
evocative, sensuous
benignly devious
disgracefully deceptive
infinitely various in
shades and emphases
raucous quarrelsome ugly
temping taunting seductive

they own no moral, but a disciplined, respect

Frank

If still alive
my father would have been
ninety-eight next month;

when Kath met him
(she remembered, too many years on)
he was Norfolk handsome,
angular, tall, deep-blue eyes,
crisp curly golden hair,
outdoor vigorous, keen;
loved the shallow Wash seas,
Broads rivers and lakes,
fishing for golden bream,
the prized catch;

few snapshots remain –
one pre-war, Prudential salesman
("sharp", grandad George said,
"got his foot in the door");
mid 1940's, smart naval officer,
later, holding our family terrier,
face, in retrospect, already
too deeply lined;

I seven, David four
when he "signed on
for the duration" of the war,
abroad a year continuously,
often ill;
before and after that

scanty home leaves
before he was "demobbed"
in a comic, ill-fitting
salt-and-pepper suit;

followed (from me)
fairly ungracious teenage years,
while he worked all hours
to overtake time lost;

for me, university
(first generation – target he
aspiring, but modest-undervaluing,
scarcely believed
within the grasp
of his family origins)

but his lot was lung cancer,
long suffering, agonising death;

I realise now I hardly knew him,
was, by reason and unreason of age,
unable to let him know me –
like our flickering movies
and scratchy gramophone,
I recall him mainly
in isolated, unconnected moments;

.... as when, one dusk in his last year,
he suggested we walk the dog,
and talked, trying to connect – "not afraid of
death ...inevitable, seen it in war ..
dishonest to claim
not to fear the process..
have contemplated hard ... don't believe
there's anything after ..must all
find our own ways to bear that ..."

how, I cry out at myself now,
can I have been so unable
to find any matching words?

he must have hoped for
some degree of perception,
comfort, some way of bridging ...
but I could not articulate it:

he will have understood
and forgiven
and been disappointed

Boyhood Fishing

In the pattern of irrigation dykes,
crossword grid of the black fens,
among tangled weed-beds lurked
fish more various than the wet-shop's slab
in the village High Street –

shoals of tiny dace an expert can lure
with a pinhead of paste
and draw out on the merest dip
of the lightest float
(dusk best hour, two or three of us
hunched under a road bridge,
gripped by the fascination of it,
knowing every passing moment
breached our curfew, wrath at home)

a rare large chub, camouflaged
three feet down,
hanging unmoving for most of an hour,
at last silver-red swirl charging the bait,
then his plump bright scales on the bank;

old pike, some as long as
George Clark's walking stick,
motionless,
endlessly patient until hungry to kill,
their sucking sounds
eerie over the flat fields, rarely caught,
and their back-set teeth
lethal as badgers';

bream lurking in deep holes;

(occasionally an adder
winding sinuous messages
along the water surface)

eels coiled in warmer water
by the pumping house
that pulsed small tides
from the New Bedford river
into the dyke system;
once we hauled out a rarity,
huge black strangely torpid,
half-fearfully carried it home
reef-knotted on bike handlebars;

perch, spiky erect dorsals,
dashing in to intercept
spoons and spinners,
shark-like turbulence;

humble, almost inedible roach,
rare tench suckering to the bottom,
rainbow trout;

hunter-gatherings
of carefree days.

War and Before

In the late thirties we were suburban:
new semi-detached, ribbon development,
on a long road with fields behind,
respectably clear of the outdated village,
short tram ride from Town facilities –
swimming-pool, skate-rink, proper shops.

Dad sold insurance to farmers,
hard graft;
often home just before bedtime –
making wonderful plasticine animals
stroll along the mantleshelf,
elephants, tigers, cobras and monkeys,
seemed there was nothing
he couldn't work out of his head.
Mother kept house, respectable.
On Sundays, affectionately hand-in-hand,
they took us, properly dressed,
for a well-behaved walk,
modestly proud of rising middle-class success.

When Dad volunteered for war
we moved, for family support,
security from city air raids
(Coventry flared on the skyline),
renting a big, draughty house
in the long fen village of mother's birth
that rose a very few feet
above Hereward's marshes.

High Street, the Row
(socially down the hill,
then, but commuter country now),
essential shops, blacksmith, woodyard,
a dozen pubs, church, two chapels.

Hastily constructed airfield
from which bombers, overloaded,
clawed into the air by small margins
over our house,
their sorties nightly counted out and back
on private short-wave radios –
always fewer returning than left.

Railway station visited
infrequently by the Grunty Fen Express,
few passengers, mainly
taking village garden produce,
worth a few pence, to London.

Sutton in the Isle
but not suburban, much rawer,
village school playground
a maelstrom –
pinch-faced girls, who shared at home
their mothers' realities,
scorned boys and let them know it;
feuding ol' boys from street clans
fomenting single combats
in yelling rings,
fen kids brought some miles to school
in an open truck;

village families sharply aware
of established local hierarchy;
anarchic London refugees
disorientated by lack of lights,
family warmth, street life,
wrote sinfully rude words
in the Church register
and were well beaten for it,
tough kids, self-contained –
improbable heroes;
a minority enclave
housed in meagre poverty
"down the Greenhills" in small
cold cottages with awful drains –
persecuted in unthinking ways.

It was a social mix that,
from my low and limited
perspective, tumultuously
challenged an historic
view of English village life.

Kath

In her last decade, my mother
would often say, sitting
in her upstairs living room
overlooking the fens towards
Haddenham's low hill
across chequer board fields,
"It's been a lovely day";
under the wide lowland skies
often the sun shines for long hours
out of cloudless, benevolent skies;
and she was contented
with her long and kindly, devoted life.

Eldest daughter and second child
in Kate's big family, to her fell
expected duties to the brood of sisters –
but her brother Bill and she
were close allies and mates;
hard now to envisage her
a pretty girl growing up in the intense
unsophistication of that inward-looking village,
where her father remarkably
owned a car and was a man of
well-concealed substance;
I recall her recalling how
in a strict household,
Bill sat on the front step
waiting until she came home from courting
covering for her lateness.

Bill was a reluctant butcher,
pressed into his father's trade,
and since the shop was a front room
in George's house, always under the eye;
he rose every day at 5 am
to make sausages in the cellar,
ever bitterly cold, with a grating
high up the wall into the yard;
Bill revelled in football and cricket -
a lean, small agile man -
coming home after every match he played
to tell his sisters: "best man on the field!"
He detested the process but
slaughtered pigs in the yard
stunning with a bolt-gun,
slitting their throats;
during the war, he sometimes took me
in his van up the long fen
farm tracks to deliver the pork
and every farmer's wife
would slip me chops
or chitterlings to take home
because of the meat rationing:
and Bill would reminisce,
 "when I were a young 'un
I was so welcome up some o' them lanes
I sometimes didn't get back for hours".

Mother had tough times:

when Frank went to Oxford
for his cancer operation –
she couldn't readily visit,
had not then learned to drive –
came back from the village phone box,
exultant almost and relieved,
to tell us "It went well,
they think he'll recover",
truth was he'd only emerged
from the anaesthetic, not much done;

after he'd died, she sold his car,
reviewed her sparse finances,
went to consult our headteacher
(a gentleman who said no
to every hint at change,
benevolently knew every pupil):
"You're still *comparatively* young,
and fit," he told her. "Must see your
boys through University.
No qualifications, but you were
an apprentice teacher once,
and there's sure to be a post
as uncertificated infant teacher
in a rural school."

I despair to remember
how far she daily travelled
to work often unwelcomed,
grossly underpaid, to support us.

Easter Piglet

Family bought an in-pig gilt,
Large White that grew to twenty score,
fed it up for its first farrowing;

combines were new then –
in late summer all local kids
were part of the ring keeping watch
at wheat harvest
as the circling machine
closed in on the centre
where rabbits gathered
until they had to break cover
and we reaped that harvest too;

our hens went broody in fold-units
under which rats lurked, which -
when we moved on these mobile homes –
were exposed, run down, despatched
by eager lethal Kim,
our mongrel, whose dream obsession
was to kill our outside cat
which reigned over its mouse kingdom
in an upstairs feed-store –
but he never exhausted its lives.

Gilt duly delivered thirteen,
suckling them noisily and often
in great family contentment,
until (less than a week on)
one piglet squeezed under the pen door
and, when challenged, showed his heels;
pursuing for miles cross-country
we were left in a flounder
by his straight-line, hedge-crashing tactics;

assuming we were now twelve,
darkness, we lit our gas mantles,
dog snored in the hearth;

hours later, faint rap at back door -
prodigal had returned, was
reintroduced to stye, burrowed under straw,
invisible, unmoving, surely had died:

on the third day he rose again
and thrived.

Grandma

Kate Clark,
gentlest of all the kindest I have known,
as near sainthood
as any person should attain,
devout Methodist who bore
five daughters and two sons
to George, farmer of few but enough
black acres (and village butcher)
to found and support his branch
of a dynasty to reckon with;

fearful of thunderstorms,
not above cheating at rummy -
but flagrant economy with the rules
of any game has been a sinfully creative
gene in most members of our family -
always signed The Pledge,
but especially in later life
kept a precautionary medicinal
store of brandy in a hat box;
dispensed a constant flow of
nourishing broth to villagers distressed;
her daily life turned on
churning rich Jersey milk
(with its sulphurous stink)
until golden flecks separated,
coalesced and were pattened
into blocks of farmhouse butter;
and pushing surreptitious

bags of sausages
into our cycle saddlebags
to ease the rationing;

she long suffered
guilt and shame sadness
that Jack, her youngest,
was simple (and spent
his later years in a home);

when, in the medical terms of those days,
she became "worn out",
her doctor told her daughters
how sad he found it
that she could not die easy
as she ought
but fretted.

To Boldly Drive

Each Spring, on our front drive,
Dad "decarbed" the engine
of our Morris Thousand -
he changed the old car in August
for a new same model
annually, for a hundred pounds all-in
at the village garage -
removed the battery,
took off the cylinder head
stripped out valves
unscrewed spark-plugs,
spread springs, washers, sundry parts
round about,
chipped off carbon deposit, reassembled all.
It was a wonder, not least because
there were always unidentified spare parts
never reincorporated

but, at a touch, the engine lived again;

southwest holidays, huge journeys
to where they'd honeymooned:
car had to be infallible
overweighted with family baggage,
temperature-running kids
… and it wasn't-failed often:
scaled Porlock after only three attempts;
was pushed groaning,
coaxed and revived in roadside crises -
return to harbour near miraculous.

During the war we "put it up"
literally – Dad going away, no other driver,
he built brick ramps under the axles,
took off the wheels
to prevent tyre perish,
drained off all fluids:
and there it was poised
in a dusty shed for three years.

Meanwhile we rode bicycles –
sit-up-and-beg primitives:
how many puncture patches,
bent spokes, twisted peddles,
undefinable grinding noises
did we conquer, or ignore?
Our lifeline though to
ride to Ely to the movies,
gather blackberries, go fishing;
aircrews on the drome
used them in thousands.

And when the church bells
wonderfully rang out the war's end,
and men came home
… Dad cranked the engine once,
it snorted and fired.

Grandson James

New-borns are always
a shocking surprise to elders
who come to pay homage
to the recurring, vital miracle
of consanguine continuity;
impossible to preconceive,
other than generally,
the specifics bound into
this bright new face,
capsule on the launch pad now
but certain to blast off
into unenvisionable outer spaces
of his own time warps.

So James, I could say to you -
"Be the free spirit
you are born to be:
judge, as only you best may, when
to stand off from the enemy
when to slip inside his guard;
be both resolute and merciful
for both are necessary;
be generous when you can" ....
and other sage advice ...

but Prince Hamlet gained only
dramatic death from his complexities
despite his Renaissance education,
and I choose not to volunteer
to be stabbed behind any arras.

This is the "one other" poem, written by Denise

All Things Lovely

The day I went to hospital
should have been routine,
but I, lazily laid back,
had left it too late;
one hospital demurred,
the second offered hope.

Do you remember driving me there,
a frost-lovely day?
The lanes white-dusted;
each grass blade encrusted, defiantly erect,
though teasel-heads hung heavily,
hoar-white with shame.

Yellow, kissing gorse flowers
mocked their dead-brown stems,
and peered through labyrinthine
spiders' webs, rough rope-woven.
A sun-russeted mouse
flashed across the road.
A kestrel, on unattached suspension,
hung motionless above the lane;
what struck me most as it slid away,
was its startling blue.

Why ever did I imagine kestrels
uniformly brown?
And how do lapwings explode from
small, black-white, cock-crested,
ground-scuttling birds, to
huge, square-winged, free-falling
tumbling clowns of the sky?

Hospital memories have faded:
these remain.

Bernard Baxter

About The Author

Bernard Baxter (b 1933) was educated at several secondary schools, remembering with particular gratitude his years at Towcester Grammar School, Northants. He took University degrees and a professional teaching qualification at Nottingham and Leeds Universities, meeting Denise, his wife of 50 years, at the latter. He describes his university years as "a freedom and a discipline totally wonderful". He played every sport available, particularly Rugby Union (and especially remembers years in the 1950's when he was privileged to play in the great Northampton Saints sides of that era). He also had a brief and glorious adventure into Boxing as a heavyweight. His professional career in teaching took him to excellent schools – Temple Moor GS in Leeds, Sale Boys' GS in Sale, Gateway GS in Leicester, Shirebrook Comprehensive in coal-mining Derbyshire – and then as its first Headteacher to open Longbenton Comprehensive High School in North Tyneside, going on to be Head of Gosforth Comprehensive High School. He subsequently worked in the School of Education at Newcastle University. He was Chief External Examiner for Didsbury College of Education and Manchester Polytechnic Teacher Training Courses. He was deeply involved in the magistracy for thirty fascinating years, and awarded the OBE. He is, he says, a maverick academic for whom English poetry is an abiding passion.

ISBN 141209193-4

9 781412 091930